Light of the World Daily Devotions

Daily Devotions, Volume 5

Dr Andrew C S Koh

Published by Dr. Andrew C S Koh, 2023.

Copyright

While every precaution has been taken in the preparation of this book, the publisher assumes no responsibility for errors or omissions, or for damages resulting from the use of the information contained herein.

LIGHT OF THE WORLD DAILY DEVOTIONS

First edition. May 28, 2023.

Copyright © 2023 Dr Andrew C S Koh.

ISBN: 979-8215331989

Written by Dr Andrew C S Koh.

Table of Contents

Dedicated to my wife, sons, daughters-in-law, grandsons, granddaughters, and to the glory of God.

Preface

Light of the World is a unique 20-day devotional book. Each day's devotion contains a selected scripture, then provides a commentary on the verses for readers to gain a fuller knowledge of God's Word. Applying the scripture to daily life is then presented in a devotional style, followed by a prayer.

This devotional is designed to deepen your relationship with God and inspire you to live a life that glorifies Him. Each daily reading includes a Bible verse, a reflection, and a prayer. The devotional covers a variety of topics, including faith, hope, love, forgiveness, and perseverance. It offers practical guidance for navigating the challenges of daily life and encourages you to trust in God's goodness and faithfulness. Whether you are a new Christian or have been walking with God for years, this devotional will help you grow in your faith and draw closer to Him each day.

Light of the World will spiritually nourish readers as they wander through the wilderness of a lost and fallen world, just as manna provided the Israelites with daily sustenance for 40 years in the wilderness.

Dr. Andrew C S Koh

1 DAY ONE

The binding of Isaac

Setting

The Hebrew word for the binding of Isaac is Akedah. This was the ultimate test for Abraham. After waiting patiently for 25 years, the LORD commanded Abraham to offer Isaac as a sacrifice! Abraham passed the test with flying colors.

The LORD called Abraham by name and commanded him to take Isaac his only son, whom he loved, and go to Moriah. The name Moriah has a beautiful meaning in Hebrew - it signifies being handpicked by God. Moriah was mentioned only twice in the Bible, and this was the first mention.

With Isaac carrying the wood, Abraham took a journey to Mount Moriah. The wood on Isaac's back was a foreshadow of the cross behind Jesus' back.

Genesis 22:9-14

9 They came to the place which God had told him of. Abraham built the altar there and laid the wood in order, bound Isaac his son, and laid him on the altar, on the wood. 10 Abraham stretched out his hand and took the knife to kill his son. 11 Yahweh's angel called to him out of the sky, and said, "Abraham, Abraham!" He said, "Here I am." 12 He said, "Don't lay your hand on the boy or do anything to him. For now, I know that you fear God since you have not withheld your son, your only son, from me." 13 Abraham lifted up his eyes and looked and saw that behind him was a ram caught in the thicket by his horns. Abraham went and took the ram and offered him up for a burnt offering instead of his son. 14 Abraham called the name of that place "Yahweh Will Provide". As it is said to this day, "On Yahweh's mountain, it will be provided."

Reflection

The angel of the LORD called Abraham by name twice and stopped him from stabbing his son. Scholars believed that this Angel of the Lord was a Christophany of the pre-incarnate Christ.

Abraham passed the test with flying colors. He obeyed the LORD's command. God provided a sacrificial ram trapped in the bush, just at the right moment. Abraham sacrificed the ram as a burnt offering to God. Abraham called Mount Moriah, Jehovah Jireh, which in Hebrews means the Lord will provide.

Because of Abraham's faith and obedience, God promised Abraham, posterity, as numerous as the stars of heaven and the sand on the seashore. The whole world will be blessed by Abraham's ultimate descendant Jesus Christ.

Application

Abraham is a type of God the Father. Isaac is a type of Jesus Christ, the only begotten Son of God.

Mount Moriah is Calvary.

On Good Friday, two thousand years ago, God provided Jesus Christ, the Lamb of God, for the sins of the world on Mount Moriah.

Whoever believes in Christ shall not perish but have eternal life, John 3:16.

Do you believe that Jesus Christ died for you on the cross 2000 years ago?

Prayer

Heavenly Father, thank You for sending Your Son Jesus Christ to die on the cross 2000 years ago to save us from sin. Thank You for salvation by grace through faith in Christ. Thank you for sanctification and eternal life, in Jesus' name, Amen.

2 DAY TWO

Judging others

Setting

Matthew 7 is a continuation of Jesus' sermon on the Mount with teachings on judging, spiritual discernment, relationship, and wisdom.

Matthew 7:1-5

1 Don't judge, so that you won't be judged. 2 For with whatever judgment you judge, you will be judged; and with whatever measure you measure, it will be measured to you. 3 Why do you see the speck that is in your brother's eye, but don't consider the beam that is in your own eye? 4 Or how will you tell your brother, 'Let me remove the speck from your eye,' and behold, the beam is in your own eye? 5 You hypocrite! First, remove the beam out of your own eye, and then you can see clearly to remove the speck out of your brother's eye.

Reflection

We cannot judge other people because we are sinners under God's judgment, Romans 3:22. If we judge we are like pots calling kettles black. We cannot judge others rightoheszly because we are not righteous. If we judge others, God will judge us.

Jesus asked two rhetorical questions. These are questions to emphasize a point and do not require any answers.

Why are we so fast to see a speck of sawdust in our brother's eye but could see the log of wood in our eye? eyes? How can we remove the speck of sawdust in our brother's eye when our vision is blocked by a log in our eye?

Romans 3:23, for all have sinned, and fall short of the glory of God.

Application

These are practical instructions to obey and apply.

Do not be a hypocrite. Remove the log in your eye first before trying to remove the speck of sawdust in your brother's eyes. Examine yourself first. Are you perfect? Are you qualified to judge?

Confess your sin before God, repent, and ask God to forgive you. Claim the promise of 1 John 1:9,

Do not take the law into your own hands. Let God be the judge Instead of judging others. Forgive others as God has forgiven you. Do not take vengeance on others. Let God deal with it.

1 John 1:9, If we confess our sins, he is faithful and righteous to forgive us the sins and to cleanse us from all unrighteousness.

Prayer

Heavenly Father, help us not to be judgmental and self-righteous. Thank You for reminding us that we are sinners under Your judgment. Thank You for redemption, reconciliation, forgiveness of sins, justification, sanctification, and salvation, in Jesus' name, Amen

3 DAY THREE

Prayer

Matthew 7:6-11

6 Don't give that which is holy to the dogs, neither throw your pearls before the pigs, lest perhaps they trample them under their feet, and turn and tear you to pieces. 7 Ask, and it will be given you. Seek, and you will find. Knock, and it will be opened for you. 8 For everyone who asks receives. He who seeks finds. To him who knocks it will be opened. 9 Or who is there among you who, if his son asks him for bread, will give him a stone? 10 Or if he asks for a fish, who will give him a serpent? 11 If you then, being evil, know how to give good gifts to your children, how much more will your Father who is in heaven give good things to those who ask him!

Reflection

We should not give valuable things to people who do not appreciate them. For example, if we give flowers to monkeys, they will trample on them and tear them to pieces in no time. This is a call for spiritual discernment and wisdom. Sharing the gospel with those who ridicule and blaspheme God is like throwing pearls to dogs.

Prayer is asking, seeking, and knocking on closed doors.

Prayer is to ask until God gives, seek until God reveals, and knock until God opens the door, Revelation:20. We must pray consistently, continuously, patiently, persistently, with perseverance, and determination. We should not allow obstacles to deter, discourage, or hinder us from prayer.

Prayer is like children asking their father for the things they need. We go to God our heavenly Father in prayer and ask Him for things that we need. If we know how to give good things to our children when they ask, God will give good things to us when we pray according to His will. His answer may be yes, no, or wait but will always be the best for us.

Application

If we who are sinful know how to give good things to our children when they ask us, how much will God give to us when we ask Him?

God is just a prayer away. Pray with faith, conviction, persistence, and perseverance. Do not throw in the towel If the answer does not come. God hears every word that you prayed. God may answer yes, no, or wait. God's answer is always the best. God is never late. He is always on time. Sometimes you have to fast and pray.

Prayer

Heavenly Father, we pray for divine enablement to pray with faith and conviction to overcome the fear of man through prayer. We pray for the gift of evangelism, in Jesus' name, Amen.

4 DAY FOUR

Beware of false prophets

Setting

In Matthew 7:12-14, Jesus gave us the golden rule, do to others what you want others to do to us and be kind to others if you want others to be kind to us. Jesus explained that He is the only way to God and the gate to salvation. After this, He warned us against false prophets.

Matthew 7:15-20

15 "Beware of false prophets, who come to you in sheep's clothing, but inwardly are ravening wolves. 16 By their fruits you will know them. Do you gather grapes from thorns or figs from thistles? 17 Even so, every good tree produces good fruit, but the corrupt tree produces evil fruit. 18 A good tree can't produce evil fruit, neither can a corrupt tree produce good fruit. 19 Every tree that doesn't grow good fruit is cut down and thrown into the fire. 20 Therefore by their fruits you will know them.

Reflection

Jesus warned us to watch out for false prophets who peddle false doctrines to lead people astray. They masquerade as sheep in wolf's clothing to deceive people with heretic teachings. They misused the gospel for personal enrichment and financial gains. False prophets were plentiful in the first-century world and even today.

We can detect false teachers by inspecting their fruits. A good tree produces good fruit. A bad tree produces bad fruit. Examine every teacher for the fruit of the spirits. Genuine teachers will have the fruit of the Spirit. Galatians 5:22-23.

Galatians 5:22-23, But the fruit of the Spirit is love, joy, peace, patience, kindness, goodness, faith, gentleness, and self-control. Against such things, there is no law.

Application

This passage is very relevant to us today because there are so many false teachers today masquerading as sheep among wolves.

Do not believe everything you hear or read. Countercheck everything you hear or read with the scriptures. Learn the Bible and be biblically literate. This is the best safeguard against heresy.

Prayer

Heavenly Father, we pray for impartation and revelation of truth. We pray for the nourishment and strengthening of our souls. We pray for maturity in faith, in Jesus' name, Amen.

5 DAY FIVE

Wise and foolish people

Matthew 7:24-29

24 "Everyone therefore who hears these words of mine and does them, I will liken him to a wise man who built his house on a rock. 25 The rain came down, the floods came, and the winds blew and beat on that house; and it didn't fall, for it was founded on the rock. 26 Everyone who hears these words of mine and doesn't do them will be like a foolish man who built his house on the sand. 27 The rain came down, the floods came, and the winds blew and beat on that house; and it fell—and its fall was great."28 When Jesus had finished saying these things, the multitudes were astonished at his teaching, 29 for he taught them with authority, and not like the scribes.

Reflections

There are two kinds of people and two types of houses. Wise people who build their houses with Jesus as the foundation will be able to withstand the onslaught of trials and persecution. Foolish people who build their houses with sand as the foundation will be washed away by floods, storms, and natural disasters. When the multitude heard these sayings, they were amazed because Jesus taught with authority, unlike the Pharisees and scribes.

Application

Praying is asking, seeking, and knocking on God. The Greek verbs, ask, seek, and knock is in the present, active, and imperative tense. This is a continuous action i.e. go on asking, go on seeking, and go on knocking. Prayer involves persistence, perseverance, and determination.

We must avoid hypocritical, judgmental, and self-righteous attitudes. We must discern false teachers by inspecting their fruits. We must build the foundation of our faith in Christ the solid rock through faith and obedience.

Prayer:

Heavenly Father, thank You for Your teaching on judging, spiritual discernment, relationship, and wisdom. Help us to build our faith with Jesus as our foundation to withstand the storms of life. Help us to go on asking, seeking, and knocking on You in prayer with persistence, perseverance, and determination, in Jesus' name, Amen.

6 DAY SIX

The feast of tabernacle

Prayer

Heavenly Father, we pray for soft, responsive, and receptive hearts to hear You speak to us. We pray for the transformation of our hearts and minds, in Jesus' name, Amen.

Setting

Jesus left Judea and came to Galilee because the Jewish religious rulers were plotting to kill Him. The Israelites were celebrating the feast of Tabernacles for 8 days. This feast commemorates the 40 years of wilderness wandering. The highlight of the feast was the water ceremony on the last day.

John 7:27-39

37 Now on the last and greatest day of the feast, Jesus stood and cried out, "If anyone is thirsty, let him come to me and drink! 38 He who believes in me, as the Scripture has said, from within him will flow rivers of living water." 39 But he said this about the Spirit, which those believing in him were to receive. For the Holy Spirit was not yet given, because Jesus wasn't yet glorified.

Reflection

On the last day of the feast, the priest performed the water ceremony. The priest took water from the pool of Siloam with a golden pitcher, walked around the altar 7 times, and poured the water to the altar of sacrifice. Just as he was pouring out the water, Jesus declared in a loud voice, "Let anyone who is thirsty come to me and drink. Whoever believes in me, as Scripture has said, rivers of living water will flow from within them." The living represents the Holy Spirit. The water ceremony re-enacted water gushing out of the rock during the wilderness wandering, Exodus 17:6. The rock was a foreshadow of Jesus.

Exodus 17:6, "Behold, I will stand before you there on the rock in Horeb, and you shall strike the rock, and water will come out of it, that the people may drink. And Moses did so in the sight of the elders of Israel."

Application:

If you want to receive Jesus as your Lord and Saviour, you need to come to Him and drink from Him. You must respond to His invitation. To drink is to believe in Him. This promise is universal. If you believe, you will be filled with the Holy Spirit and He will overflow out of you to others.

Matthew 11:28, "Come to Me, all you who labor and are heavy laden, and I will give you rest."

Prayer:

Dear God, we believe that Jesus of Nazareth is your son and our savior. He is the Messiah, the Holy One of Israel, the Living Water, the Living Bread, and the Bread of Life. In His name, we pray. Amen.

7 DAY SEVEN

15

Roll away the stone

Prayer:

Heavenly Father, thank You that You are the resurrection and the life. Thank You for Your appointment with us to speak to us through scripture, in Jesus' name, Amen.

Setting

The raising of Lazarus after 4 days in the tomb was the 7th and most significant sign in the Gospel of John. By now, Lazarus' body had undergone irreversible decay and decomposition. The Jews questioned Jesus' inability to prevent Lazarus' death. Jesus demanded to roll back the stone, but Marta objected saying, "Lord, by now it stinkered" (KJV). In the first-century world, the Jews buried their dead in caves. After wrapping the corpse with linens from head to toe, and burying it inside the tomb, they will roll a large round stone across the entrance. After many months, relatives of the dead person will collect the bones and store them in a stone box called an ossuary.

John 11:40-44

40 Jesus said to her, "Didn't I tell you that if you believed, you would see God's glory?" 41 So they took away the stone from the place where the dead man was lying. Jesus lifted up his eyes, and said, "Father, I thank you that you listened to me. 42 I know that you always listen to me, but because of the multitude standing around I said this, that they may believe that you sent me." 43 When he had said this, he cried with a loud voice, "Lazarus, come out!" 44 He who was dead came out, bound hand and foot with wrappings, and his face was wrapped around with a cloth. Jesus said to them, "Free him, and let him go."

Reflection

Jesus told Marta to believe. Jesus prayed to His Father in a loud voice, "Lazarus come out". Lazarus came out wrapped in the grave linens. Jesus said, remove the grave linens and set him free. When Jesus rose from death, His body passed through the grave linens like a butterfly coming out of a cocoon. The Resurrected Christ was raised to eternal life. Lazarus was raised to natural life and would eventually die again. Christians will be resurrected to eternal life in the rapture, 1 Thessalonians 4:16.

1 Thessalonians 4:16, "For the Lord himself will come down from heaven, with a loud command, with the voice of the archangel and with the trumpet call of God, and the dead in Christ will rise first".

Application

The raising of Lazarus was not an ordinary miracle. After 4 days in the tomb, Lazarus was dead beyond any shadow of a doubt.

The raising of Lazarus was a prelude to the resurrection of Jesus.

The raising of Lazarus was also a prelude to the rapture when all Christians, whether alive or dead, will be raised from the dead to meet Christ as He descends from heaven. Jesus is the resurrection and the life. Whoever believes in Him will have eternal life.

Prayer

Heavenly Father, thank You for the gift of eternal life. We thank You for the promise of resurrection for those who believe in You. Thank You that while we were still sinners, Christ died for us, in Jesus' name, Amen

8 DAY EIGHT

God's magnificent throne

Setting

After recording the letters to the seven churches of Revelation, John was raptured to heaven through an out-of-body spiritual experience. He entered an opened door and heard a voice speaking to him. He saw God sitting on His throne, built with green jasper and red sardius gemstones. The throne was surrounded by a green, emerald rainbow.

Revelation 4:4-8

4 Around the throne were twenty-four thrones. On the thrones were twenty-four elders sitting, dressed in white garments, with crowns of gold on their heads. 5 Out of the throne proceed lightning, sounds, and thunders. There were seven lamps of fire burning before his throne, which are the seven Spirits of God. 6 Before the throne was something like a sea of glass, similar to crystal. In the middle of the throne, and around the throne were four living creatures full of eyes before and behind. 7 The first creature was like a lion, the second creature like a calf, and the third creature had a face like a man, and the fourth was like a flying eagle. 8 The four living creatures, each one of them having six wings, are full of eyes around and within. They have no rest day and night, saying, "Holy, holy, holy is the Lord God, the Almighty, who was and who is and who is to come!"

Reflection:

God's throne was surrounded by 24 thrones occupied by 24 elders, dressed in white, and crowned with golden crowns. John heard lightning and thunder and saw 7 menorahs lit up. A sea of crystal-clear glass is in front of the throne. At the centre and periphery of the throne, John saw 4 living creatures with eyes facing forward and backward.

The first living creature was like a lion, the second an ox, the third a man, and the fourth an eagle. The emblem of Matthew's gospel is a lion, Mark, an ox, Luke, a man, and John, an eagle. The four living creatures had 6 wings and were full of eyes, Ezekiel 1:10-11. They continuously proclaimed Holy, Holy, Holy, 24 hours a day, and 7 days a week.

Ezekiel 1:10-11, "As for the likeness of their faces, they had the face of a man. The four of them had the face of a lion on the right side. The four of them had the face of an ox on the left side. The four of them also had the face of an eagle. Such were their faces. Their wings were spread out above. Two wings of each one touched another, and two covered their bodies."

Application:

John gave us a glimpse into God's glorious heavenly throne. This is a prelude to a future event. One day, all believers of Christ will see the glorious throne of God in heaven. Amidst the uncertainty of life, this is a promise for Christians to claim.

Prayer

Heavenly Father, thank You for giving a glimpse into Your throne room in heaven through the eyes of John. The magnificence, glory, and excellency of Your throne are beyond words, beyond language, and beyond description. You are worthy to receive glory, honor, power, and praise for You created all things, in Jesus' name, Amen

9 DAY NINE

The seven seal judgments

Setting

John saw God the Father sitting on His throne holding a book sealed on both sides with seven seals. A mighty angel invites whoever is worthy to open the book and break its seals. John wept because no one was found worthy to open the book. One of the twenty-four elders assured John that Christ, the lion of Judah, and a descendant of David was worthy to open the book.

Revelation 5:5-8

5 One of the elders said to me, "Don't weep. Behold, the Lion who is of the tribe of Judah, the Root of David, has overcome: he who opens the book and its seven seals." 6 I saw in the middle of the throne and of the four living creatures, and in the middle of the elders, a Lamb standing, as though it had been slain, having seven horns and seven eyes, which are the seven Spirits of God, sent out into all the earth. 7 Then he came, and he took it out of the right hand of him who sat on the throne. 8 Now when he had taken the book, the four living creatures and the twenty-four elders fell down before the Lamb, each one having a harp, and golden bowls full of incense, which are the prayers of the saints.

Reflection

John saw a slain Lamb with seven horns and seven eyes standing in the centre of God's throne. Seven is God's perfect and complete number. Seven horns are symbolic of Christ's perfect kingship. Seven eyes are symbolic of the seven ministries of the Holy Spirit, Isaiah 11:2. Christ took the book from the right hand of God the Father. The four living creatures and the twenty-four elders worshiped Christ by falling forward and singing praises. They played harps and proclaimed that the Lamb who was killed is worthy of power, wealth, wisdom, strength, honor, glory, and blessing." Revelation 5:12.

Application

Christ is the only person who is qualified and worthy to take the book with seven seals from the Father's hand and open them because He is holy, pure, perfect, righteous, and sinless. He, who is sinless, took our sins upon Himself on the cross to redeem us from sin and death.

Prayer

Heavenly Father, thank You for sending Jesus Christ to the world 2000 years ago to live a perfect life and died a cruel death on the cross to pay the penalty of our sins for us. Thank You that Christ is eminently qualified and worthy to take the scroll from Your hand opened them, in Jesus' name, Amen.

10 DAY TEN

22

Evangelistic preaching

Prayer:

Heavenly Father, You are Jehovah Rapha, Jehovah Rohi, Jehovah Nissi, Jehovah Jireh, Jehovah Tsidkenu, Jehovah Mkadesh, Jehovah Shamma, Jehovah Seboath, and Jehovah Shalom. You are all these and much more. Thank You for loving us and caring for us, in Jesus' name, Amen.

Setting

Paul and his team traveled to Amphipolis, Apollonian, and Thessalonica. The Jews in Thessalonica started a mob in the city to arrest Paul, but they did not find him. The disciples sent Paul and Silas to Berea by night.

Later, the Jews from Thessalonica came to Berea and started another riot there. The disciples sent Paul away to Athens by sea, leaving Silas and Timothy behind.

Paul confronted the philosophers of Athens, and they were keen to listen to Paul's teaching.

They took Paul to the Areopagus and allowed him to speak there.

When Paul was walking in the streets of Athens, he saw plenty of statues, and one particular statute was dedicated to an unknown god. Paul used this as an icebreaker for his sermon.

Acts 17:24-31

24 The God who made the world and all things in it, he, being Lord of heaven and earth, doesn't dwell in temples made with hands. 25 He isn't served by men's hands, as though he needed anything, seeing he himself gives to all life and breath, and all things. 26 He made from one blood every nation of men to dwell on all the surface of the earth, having determined appointed seasons, and the boundaries of their dwellings, 27 that they should seek the Lord if perhaps they might reach out for him and find him, though he is not far from each one of us. 28 'For in him we live, move, and have our being.' As some of your own poets have said, 'For we are also his offspring.' 29 Being then the offspring of God, we ought not to think that the Divine Nature is like gold, or silver, or stone, engraved by art and design of man. 30 The times of ignorance therefore God overlooked. But now he commands that all people everywhere should repent, 31 because he has appointed a day in which he will judge the world in righteousness by the man whom he has ordained; of which he has given assurance to all men, in that he has raised him from the dead."

Reflection

Here was Paul's evangelistic sermon. Paul quoted phrases from two Greek poets, "we live and move and have our being" and "we were also his offspring".

God is the creator and does not live in man-made temples. He gave life to all living things. He created the first human being Adam who populated the whole world. He predetermined the times and places where people will live. God is a personal God who wants our relationship. We are God's children. God is not an idol fashioned by men using gold, silver, wood, or stone. God overlooked people's ignorance in times past but now He commanded everyone to repent of their sins. God judged the world in righteousness through the Lord Jesus Christ, whom God raised from the dead to prove that He is God.

Application

Paul was a great evangelist. He used their unknown God as an icebreaker. After his sermon, some mocked, some wanted to hear more, but some believed. Paul sowed the seed of the gospel. He was not worried about the response.

You can learn from Paul. Use an icebreaker to make contact and create a rapport with your audience. Your job is to sow the seed of the Gospel. Do not worry about the response. Faith comes by hearing the word of God. Conversion is the work of the Holy Spirit, not you or me.

Prayer

Heavenly Father, help us to master the art of evangelistic preaching in the marketplace. Help us to imitate Paul just as he imitated Christ. We pray for the anointing and gifts of the Holy Spirit to equip us in ministry, in Jesus' name, Amen.

n

11 DAY ELEVEN

25

He is not here, He has risen!

Prayer

Heavenly Father, we come before You to learn, listen, worship, and fellowship with You. Speak to us and Your servants will listen, hear, and obey, in Jesus' name, Amen.

Setting

Mary Magdalene came to the tomb very early on Easter Sunday when it was still dark. She saw the tombstone rolled away and falsely concluded that tomb raiders came to steal the Lord's body. She bumped into Peter and John and told them about it. The duo were so excited, they raced to the tomb as fast as they could!

John 20:4-10

4 They both ran together. The other disciple outran Peter and came to the tomb first. 5 Stooping and looking in, he saw the linen cloths lying, yet he didn't enter in. 6 Then Simon Peter came, following him, and entered into the tomb. He saw the linen cloths lying, 7 and the cloth that had been on his head, not lying with the linen cloths, but rolled up in a place by itself. 8 So then the other disciple who came first to the tomb also entered in, and he saw and believed. 9 For as yet they didn't know the Scripture, that he must rise from the dead. 10 So the disciples went away again to their own homes.

Reflection

John outran Pater, glanced, and saw from outside the tomb. He did not go in. The Greek word for saw here is "blepo" which means to look casually. John did not see anything significant.

Peter arrived at the scene, enter the tomb, and saw the linen cloths lying on the floor, undisturbed in 2 piles, one for the head, and one for the rest of the body from the neck to the toes. The Greek word for saw here is "theoreo", which means to see like a detective investigating a crime scene. Peter saw the empty tomb but could not connect the dots.

After this, John enter the tomb and saw what Peter had seen. The Greek word for saw here is "aido", which means to see with insight and understanding. John saw the "cocoon" and correctly concluded that Jesus had resurrected from the dead. He understood that Christ's body had passed out from the linen cloths like a butterfly exiting a cocoon. John was the first disciple to believe in the Resurrection.

On Good Friday, Joseph of Arimathea and Nicodemus wrapped up Jesus' body with linen strips from the head to the toes. The linen strips were interlaced with myrrh and aloes for embalming. When the spices dried up, the linen strips hardened and solidified into a cocoon-like structure.

Application:

On Easter, three people came out with different opinions. Mary saw the open grave and concluded the tomb raiders had stolen the body. Peter saw but could not connect the dots. John saw and believed that Christ had Risen. What about you? What did you 'see' from the Easter narrative? Will you see the Risen Christ and believe?

You can now go to the garden tomb in Jerusalem and feel the same as Peter and John did when they found the tomb empty. It's a great place for a pilgrimage. The Bible is about real people, real events, real history, and real geography. It is not a figment of someone's imagination. The Bible is the inspired Word of God.

Prayer:

Heavenly Father, thank You for Good Friday and Easter Sunday. Thank You that You have conquered sin and death on Good Friday and rose from the grave on Easter. Thank You for the gift of salvation and eternal life, in Jesus' name, Amen.

12 DAY TWELVE

28

Beatitudes

Setting

The sermon on the Mount, from Matthew 5 to 7 is Christ's manifesto for Christian discipleship and kingdom living. The sermon on the Mount begins with a series of eight beatitudes or blessings from Matthew 5:1-12. Latin for beatitude is beatitudo, which means, blessedness.

Matthew 5:1-12

1 Seeing the multitudes, he went up onto the mountain. When he had sat down, his disciples came to him. 2 He opened his mouth and taught them, saying, 3 "Blessed are the poor in spirit, for theirs is the Kingdom of Heaven. Isaiah 57:15; 66:2. 4 Blessed are those who mourn, for they shall be comforted. Isaiah 61:2; 66:10,13. 5 Blessed are the gentle, for they shall inherit the earth. Psalm 37:11. 6 Blessed are those who hunger and thirst for righteousness, for they shall be filled. 7 Blessed are the merciful, for they shall obtain mercy. 8 Blessed are the pure in heart, for they shall see God. 9 Blessed are the peacemakers, for they shall be called children of God. 10 Blessed are those who have been persecuted for righteousness's sake, for theirs is the Kingdom of Heaven. 11 "Blessed are you when people reproach you, persecute you, and say all kinds of evil against you falsely, for my sake. 12 Rejoice, and be exceedingly glad, for great is your reward in heaven. For that is how they persecuted the prophets who were before you.

Reflection

Jesus sat down and taught the disciples from a mountain.

These eight beatitudes set the scene and pace for the sermon on the Mount.

Blessed are those who realized how spiritually bankrupt they are before. a Holy God. They will receive the kingdom of Heaven.

Blessed are those who are sorrowful for they will be comforted.

Blessed are those who are gentle of heart for they inherit the earth.

Blessed are those who hunger and thirst for righteousness, for they shall be filled.

Blessed are those who show mercy to others, for they shall receive mercy.

Blessed are the pure in heart for they shall see God.

Blessed are the peacemakers for they shall be adopted as children of God.

Blessed are those who are persecuted for Christ's sake, for they shall be rewarded in heaven.

The Old Testament prophets who lived centuries before Christ and were persecuted for God's sake will be rewarded in heaven. Jesus quoted Isaiah 57:15, 66:2, 61:2, 66:10, 66:13, and Psalm 37:11.

Application

The beatitudes are eight attitudes that you should adopt. These are poverty in the spirit, sorrow, gentleness, hunger for what is right, merciful, purity, peacemaker, and persecution. God will reward you with eternal life in the kingdom of heaven.

Prayer

Heavenly Father, thank You for teaching us about the eight beatitudes. Thank You for spelling out to us Your manifestos for Christian discipleship and kingdom living. Help us to obey your teachings and be Holy because You are Holy, in Jesus' name, Amen.

13 DAY THIRTEEN

Salt and light

Matthew 5:13-16

13 "You are the salt of the earth, but if the salt has lost its flavor, with what will it be salted? It is then good for nothing, but to be cast out and trodden under the feet of men. 14 You are the light of the world. A city located on a hill can't be hidden. 15 Neither do you light a lamp and put it under a measuring basket, but on a stand; and it shines to all who are in the house. 16 Even so, let your light shine before men, that they may see your good works and glorify your Father who is in heaven.

Reflection

Christians are the salt of the world. Salt is a taste enhancer and a preservative. Salt is useful only if it maintains its saltiness. Christians exert their influence on the world by bringing hope to the lives of non-Christians and preserving the moral decay of society.

Christians are the night of the world. A lamp must be installed on a lamp-stand to give light to the room. It must not be hidden under a basket. Christians reflect the true light of Christ to the people living in a dark world. Christians shine their light through their testimony to glorify God.

Application

Are you a salt and light to the world? Are you salty enough to give the flavour of life to non-Christians?

Are you salty enough to preserve the moral decay of the corrupt society?

Are you shining the light of Christ to other people around you? Are you testifying the glory of God through personal testimony and evangelism?

What must you do to be the salt and light of the world?

Prayer

Heavenly Father, we come before You into Your presence with brokenness, and humility, hearts and teachable spirits. in Help us to be salt and light of the world, Jesus' name, Amen.

14 DAY FOURTEEN

. Day 14

Sermon on the Mount (1)

Setting

Jesus fulfilled the law by living a perfect sinless life that no other human being could ever do. For everyone is a sinner and a lawbreaker, Romans 3:23. Jesus the perfect man fulfilled the law for us and obtained justification for our sins. Heaven and earth will pass away but the word of God will last into eternity.

Matthew 4:27-30

27 "You have heard that it was said, 'You shall not commit adultery;' Exodus 20:14 28 but I tell you that everyone who gazes at a woman to lust after her has committed adultery with her already in his heart. 29 If your right eye causes you to stumble, pluck it out and throw it away from you. For it is more profitable for you that one of your members should perish than for your whole body to be cast into Gehenna. 30 If your right hand causes you to stumble, cut it off, and throw it away from you. For it is more profitable for you that one of your members should perish than for your whole body to be cast into Gehenna.

Reflection

The law prohibits adultery, but Jesus raised the bar even higher. To look at a woman lustfully is to commit adultery in the heart. It is better to enter heaven without eyes than to enter heaven with lustful eyes. It is better to enter heaven without a right hand than to enter heaven with a right hand that sinned. Plucking out eyes and cutting off hands is a figurative language to be interpreted figuratively.

Application

The sermon on the Mount is Jesus' manifesto for Christian discipleship and kingdom living. Jesus' standards go far beyond the law. It is not the letter of the law that counts but the spirit of the law. The law said, do not murder, but Jesus said, do not even be angry. The law said, do not commit adultery, but Jesus said, do not even look lustfully at a woman. The law said, love your neighbour, but Jesus said, love even your enemy.

Prayer

Heavenly Father, we claim the promise that Your word is a lamp to our feet and a light to our path. We claim the promise that we will know the Truth and the Truth will set us free, in Jesus' name, Amen.

n

15 DAY FIFTEEN

. Sermon on the Mount (2)

Setting

The law prohibits making false wows and abandoning wows made to God, but Jesus raised the bar higher. You should not swear before man, God, earth, and heaven. You should honour your word. Double-talk is prohibited. Mean what you say and say what you mean. There are no two ways about this.

Matthew 5: 38-41

38 "You have heard that it was said, 'An eye for an eye, and a tooth for a tooth.' Exodus 21:24; Leviticus 24:20; Deuteronomy 19:21 39 But I tell you, don't resist him who is evil; but whoever strikes you on your right cheek, turn to him the other also. 40 If anyone sues you to take away your coat, let him have your cloak also. 41 Whoever compels you to go one mile, go with him two. 42 Give to him who asks you and don't turn away him who desires to borrow from you.

Reflection

The law allowed lex talionis, repaying an eye for an eye and a tooth for a tooth. This was to prevent over-retaliation in the event of wrongdoing. Jesus raised the bar higher. When someone slaps you on one cheek, offer him the other cheek. If someone takes away your coat, offer him your tunic. If someone forced you to walk one mile, walk two miles. Give generously to people in need and lend to those who need a loan.

Application

You must not retaliate because retaliation will lead to more violence. You must take revenge because revenge belongs to God. Let God deal with the provocateurs. Be very generous to people in need. This is Christ's manifesto for kingdom living.

Godly wisdom and earthly wisdom

Prayer:

Heavenly Father, we pray for the Holy Spirit to give us wisdom, discernment, understanding, and insight into spiritual truths. We pray for our spiritual eyes to be opened and our spiritual blindness to be removed, in Jesus' name, Amen.

Setting

Paul acknowledged that he was not a great orator, but he preached the gospel and declared his testimony through the wisdom of God. Paul's priority was to preach the crucifixion of Christ. Paul acknowledged that he was trembling, fearful, and weak. He did not speak with human wisdom but through Godly wisdom and the power of the Holy Spirit. Paul relied on Godly wisdom and not human wisdom.

1 Corinthians 2:6-10

6 However, we speak wisdom among those who are mature, yet not the wisdom of this age, nor of the rulers of this age, who are coming to nothing. 7 But we speak the wisdom of God in a mystery, the hidden wisdom which God ordained before the ages for our glory, 8 which none of the rulers of this age knew; for had they known, they would not have crucified the Lord of glory. 9 But as it is written: "Eye has not seen, nor ear heard, nor have entered into the heart of man, the things which God has prepared for those who love Him." 10 But God has revealed them to us through His Spirit. For the Spirit searches all things, yes, the deep things of God.

Reflection

There are two kinds of wisdom, Godly wisdom, and human wisdom. Godly wisdom is contrary to human wisdom. Paul spoke about a mystery concerning the crucifixion and resurrection of Christ. The rulers of this age, who were ignorant of this mystery, crucified the Lord of Glory.

The Holy Spirit revealed spiritual truths to born-again Christians but not to non-Christians because they do not have the Holy Spirit. The Holy Spirit searched the hearts and minds of Christians to reveal, teach, convict, correct, instruct, and train in righteous living.

Godly wisdom comes from the Holy Spirit, human wisdom comes from men. Godly wisdom is spiritual, earthly wisdom is earthly. The "natural" men cannot understand spiritual truth because they do not have the Holy Spirit. Satan had blinded the eyes of non-Christians so that they are unable to understand the things of God.

Application:

We should seek Godly wisdom and not human wisdom. Godly wisdom comes from the Holy Spirit who searched our hearts and minds.

Non-Christians cannot understand spiritual truths because they are blinded by Satan. Before you share the gospel with non-Christians, you must pray for God to remove their spiritual blindness.

Prayer:

Heavenly Father, thank You for revealing to us the deep things of God through the Holy Spirit. Thank You for revealing spiritual truth and wisdom to us through the Holy Spirit's presence. Thank You for opening our spiritual eyes to see, know, understand, and discern spiritual truths, in Jesus' name, Amen.

16 DAY SIXTEEN

40

Godly wisdom and earthly wisdom

Prayer:

Heavenly Father, we pray for the Holy Spirit to give us wisdom, discernment, understanding, and insight into spiritual truths. We pray for our spiritual eyes to be opened and our spiritual blindness to be removed, in Jesus' name, Amen.

Setting

Paul acknowledged that he was not a great orator, but he preached the gospel and declared his testimony through the wisdom of God. Paul's priority was to preach the crucifixion of Christ. Paul acknowledged that he was trembling, fearful, and weak. He did not speak with human wisdom but through Godly wisdom and the power of the Holy Spirit. Paul relied on Godly wisdom and not human wisdom.

1 Corinthians 2:6-10

6 However, we speak wisdom among those who are mature, yet not the wisdom of this age, nor of the rulers of this age, who are coming to nothing. 7 But we speak the wisdom of God in a mystery, the hidden wisdom which God ordained before the ages for our glory, 8 which none of the rulers of this age knew; for had they known, they would not have crucified the Lord of glory. 9 But as it is written: "Eye has not seen, nor ear heard, nor have entered into the heart of man, the things which God has prepared for those who love Him." 10 But God has revealed them to us through His Spirit. For the Spirit searches all things, yes, the deep things of God.

Reflection

There are two kinds of wisdom, Godly wisdom, and human wisdom. Godly wisdom is contrary to human wisdom. Paul spoke about a mystery concerning the crucifixion and resurrection of Christ. The rulers of this age, who were ignorant of this mystery, crucified the Lord of Glory.

The Holy Spirit revealed spiritual truths to born-again Christians but not to non-Christians because they do not have the Holy Spirit. The Holy Spirit searched the hearts and minds of Christians to reveal, teach, convict, correct, instruct, and train in righteous living.

Godly wisdom comes from the Holy Spirit, human wisdom comes from men. Godly wisdom is spiritual, earthly wisdom is earthly. The "natural" men cannot understand spiritual truth because they do not have the Holy Spirit. Satan had blinded the eyes of non-Christians so that they are unable to understand the things of God.

Application:

We should seek Godly wisdom and not human wisdom. Godly wisdom comes from the Holy Spirit who searched our hearts and minds.

Non-Christians cannot understand spiritual truths because they are blinded by Satan. Before you share the gospel with non-Christians, you must pray for God to remove their spiritual blindness.

Prayer:

Heavenly Father, thank You for revealing to us the deep things of God through the Holy Spirit. Thank You for revealing spiritual truth and wisdom to us through the Holy Spirit's presence. Thank You for opening our spiritual eyes to see, know, understand, and discern spiritual truths, in Jesus' name, Amen.

.

17 DAY SEVENTEEN

Old Testament typology

Prayer

Heavenly Father, we come before You again on bended knees, with open spirits, eyes, ears, and obedient hearts. We offer our bodies to You as living sacrifices to serve You and sacrifices of praise to worship You, in Jesus' name, Amen.

Setting

Paul alluded to the Exodus story. God protected the Israelites of the Exodus with a pillar cloud in the day and a pillar of fire at night. God miraculously parted the Red Sea for them to walk on dry ground. The pillar of cloud and fire are foreshadows of the Holy Spirit. Passing through the Red Sea was a foreshadow of water baptism.

1 Corinthians 10:3-11

3 all ate the same spiritual food, 4 and all drank the same spiritual drink. For they drank of that spiritual Rock that followed them, and that Rock was Christ. 5 But with most of them God was not well pleased, for their bodies were scattered in the wilderness. 6 Now these things became our examples, to the intent that we should not lust after evil things as they also lusted. 7 And do not become idolaters as were some of them. As it is written, "The people sat down to eat and drink, and rose up to play." 8 Nor let us commit sexual immorality, as some of them did, and in one day twenty-three thousand fell; 9 nor let us tempt Christ, as some of them also tempted, and were destroyed by serpents; 10 nor complain, as some of them also complained, and were destroyed by the destroyer. 11 Now all these things happened to them as examples, and they were written for our admonition, upon

whom the ends of the ages have come.

Reflections

The Israelites ate manna and drank water from the rock. Manna and the rock are foreshadows of Christ. The water was a foreshadow of the Holy Spirit. Only Joshua and Caleb entered the promised land out of the two million Israelites who crossed the Red Sea. All the rest perished in the wilderness.

The Greek word for example is "tupos", which means type or foreshadow. These things are foreshadows of Christ. Paul warned his audience against idolatry, sexual immorality, disobedience, and grumbling against God. He quoted Exodus 32:6 and Numbers 25:9 and Numbers 21:9. The bronze serpent was a foreshadow of Christ.

Exodus 32:6, "And they rose up early on the morrow, and offered burnt offerings, and brought peace offerings; and the people sat down to eat and to drink and rose up to play."

Numbers 25:9, "And those who died in the plague were twenty-four thousand."

Numbers 21:9, "So Moses made a bronze serpent and put it on the flag pole; and it came about, that if a serpent bit someone, and he looked at the bronze serpent, he lived."

Application

The Old Testament narratives contain examples, types, or foreshadows of the New Testament truth. The Old Testament is the shadow while the New Testament is the reality. Many Old Testament personalities are types of Christ. For example, Joseph is a type of Christ. When you read the Old Testament, look out for these typologies.

Prayer

Heavenly Father, thank You that it is by grace that we have been saved through faith in Your Son Jesus Christ, and not by work. Give us the stamina, energy, strength, wisdom, persistence, and consistency to study and meditate on Your word, in Jesus' name, Amen.

18 DAY EIGHTEEN

45

overcoming temptation and Holy Communion

1 Corinthians 10:12-18.

12 Therefore let him who thinks he stands take heed lest he fall. 13 No temptation has overtaken you except such as is common to man; but God is faithful, who will not allow you to be tempted beyond what you are able, but with the temptation will also make the way of escape, that you may be able to bear it. 14 Therefore, my beloved, flee from idolatry. 15 I speak as to wise men; judge for yourselves what I say. 16 The cup of blessing which we bless, is it not the communion of the blood of Christ? The bread which we break, is it not the communion of the body of Christ? 17 For we, though many, are one bread and one body; for we all partake of that one bread.18 Observe Israel after the flesh: Are not those who eat of the sacrifices partakers of the altar?

Reflection

1 Corinthians 10:13 is a promise to claim for overcoming temptation. God will not allow us to be tempted beyond what we can bear, and He will create a way for us to overcome it.

Paul encouraged his audience to run away from idolatry. Concerning Holy Communion, Paul asked two rhetorical questions. The cup of Holy Communion represents the blood of Christ. The bread of the Holy Communion represents the body of Christ.

Application

You can claim the promise of 1 Corinthians 10:13 if you are going through temptations. God will not allow you to be tempted beyond what you can bear and will make a way for you to overcome it.

Prayer

Heavenly Father, thank You for Christ's death, burial, resurrection, glorification, and ascension to heaven. Thank You for the forgiveness of sin, the gift of salvation, and the promise of eternal life, in Jesus' name, Amen

19 DAY NINETEEN

.

Eating food offered to idols

Setting

Paul asked three rhetorical questions. Idols are not "gods" but demons. We cannot drink the cup of communion and the cup of demons. We cannot have fellowship with God and fellowship with demons or we will provoke the wrath of God.

Paul said that all things are lawful but not all things are edifying. We should look out for one another's well-being and not be a stumbling block to one another. We should eat whatever is sold in the market asking no questions for conscience's sake. Everything belonged to God.

1 Corinthians 10:27-31

27 If any of those who do not believe invites you to dinner, and you desire to go, eat whatever is set before you, asking no question for conscience' sake. 28 But if anyone says to you, "This was offered to idols," do not eat it for the sake of the one who told you, and for conscience' sake; for "the earth is the Lord's, and all its fullness." 29 "Conscience," I say, not your own, but that of the other. For why is my liberty judged by another man's conscience? 30 But if I partake with thanks, why am I evil spoken of for the food over which I give thanks? 31 Therefore, whether you eat or drink, or whatever you do, do all to the glory of God.

Reflection

When we are invited to a dinner by a non-Christian, we should eat without asking any questions. But if we are told that the food has been offered to idols, then we must not eat it for the sake of our host's conscience and for our own conscience's sake. Paul asked two rhetorical questions and concluded that whatever we eat, drink, or do, do it all for the glory of God.

Application:

You should not eat food offered to idols because this may cause a weaker Christian to stumble when they see you eat it. If your conscience does not allow you to eat it, do not.

Prayer:

Heavenly Father, help us to run away from idolatry, sexual immorality, disobedience, and murmuring against You. Help us not to eat food offered to idols so as not to be a stumbling block to weak Christians and for conscience' sake, in Jesus' name, Amen.

20 DAY TWENTY

Waiting on the Lord

Prayer:

Dear God, we trust in Your promise that Your word will always achieve its purpose. We ask this in the name of Jesus, Amen.

Setting

Christ revealed Himself to Paul on the Damascus Road and appointed him to be an apostle to the Gentiles.

Before his conversion, Paul was a zealous Pharisee who persecuted the Christians. After his conversion, he made a 180-degree U-turn to be an apostle, missionary, church planter, and evangelist. Paul isolated himself in the desert of Arabia for 3 years before returning to Damascus.

Galatians 1: 18-24,

18 Then after three years I went up to Jerusalem to visit Peter and stayed with him for fifteen days. 19 But of the other apostles I saw no one except James, the Lord's brother. 20 Now about the things which I write to you, behold, before God, I'm not lying. 21 Then I came to the regions of Syria and Cilicia. 22 I was still unknown by face to the assemblies of Judea which were in Christ, 23 but they only heard: "He who once persecuted us now preaches the faith that he once tried to destroy." 24 So they glorified God in me.

Reflection

After his conversion, Paul spent 3 years in the Arabian desert alone waiting upon the Lord. After this, Paul went up to Jerusalem and there, Peter gave him a Bible study for fifteen days. He also met the Lord's half-brother, James, but did not meet any of the other apostles. Paul testified before God that he was telling the truth.

After returning from Arabia, Paul went to Syria and then to Tarsus, Cilicia, his hometown. The Christians in Judea never met Paul but knew that he was once a Christian persecutor. When they heard Paul's testimony, they glorified God. Paul spent another 14 years in Tarsus and waiting upon the Lord.

Application:

Paul waited on the Lord for 17 years before God called him to minister at Antioch. He was in Arabia for 3 years and in Tarsus for 14 years. Waiting is an essential component of discipleship. Waiting is essential for preparation, faith, maturity, humility, solitude, patience, perseverance, and training in righteousness. Moses waited 40 years before God called him to lead the Israelites out of Egypt. Joseph waited 15 years before God promoted him to be the Prime Minister of Egypt. Abraham waited 25 years before God gave him Isaac. Do not worry if you are waiting because you are under God's training. God's timing is never too early or too late. His timing is perfect. By waiting, your faith will be strengthened, and you will encounter spiritual breakthroughs.

Prayer

Heavenly Father, we claim the promise that those who wait on You will renew their strength and soar on the wings of eagles. They shall run and not be weary, and they shall run and not faint, in Jesus' name, Amen.

ONE LAST THING

Please consider writing a review of my book. Your feedback is valuable to me and can help other potential readers decide whether to pick up a copy. If you enjoyed the book, it would mean the world to me if you could leave a positive review on Goodreads or Bookbub. If you have any constructive criticism, I am also open to hearing it, as it can help me improve my writing. Thank you for taking the time to read my work, and I hope to hear from you soon!

Dr. Andrew C S Koh

Don't miss out!

Visit the website below and you can sign up to receive emails whenever Dr Andrew C S Koh publishes a new book. There's no charge and no obligation.

https://books2read.com/r/B-A-FMXV-AASJC

BOOKS2READ

Connecting independent readers to independent writers.

Did you love *Light of the World Daily Devotions*? Then you should read *Bread of Life Daily Devotions*[1] by Dr Andrew C S Koh!

Bread of Life is a unique 20-day devotional book. Each day's devotion contains a selected scripture, a commentary on the verses, and the application of the scripture to daily life, followed by a prayer. The selected Scripture verses are taken from the entire Bible, providing a wonderful overview of the basic doctrines of the Christian faith. This novel will provide a strong foundation for new believers to start building their journey of faith and walking with Christ. For mature saints, this book provides spiritual nourishment and refreshment. Just as manna provided the Israelites with daily nourishment in the wilderness, Bread of Life will provide readers with spiritual nourishment in the wilderness of life.

Read more at https://www.drandrewcskoh.com.

---

1. https://books2read.com/u/mZ0Bv5

2. https://books2read.com/u/mZ0Bv5

Also by Dr Andrew C S Koh

Daily Devotion
Manna of Life: Daily Devotion

Daily Devotions
Bread of Life Daily Devotions
Words of Eternal Life
Bread From Heaven: Daily Devotions
Light of the World Daily Devotions
Light of the World Daily Devotions

Genesis
Understanding Genesis 1-11: From Adam to Abraham
Faith Journey of Abraham: Genesis 12-25
Life Story of Jacob: Genesis 26-36
Life of Joseph: Genesis 37-50

Gospels and Act
The Gospel According to Matthew
Daily Devotion Gospel of Mark
The Gospel According to Luke
Daily Devotion Gospel of John

Acts: Volume 1 and 2, From Jerusalem to Rome

Non Pauline and General Epistles
Hebrews: the Just Shall Live by Faith
1 John, 2 John, 3 John & Jude: a Verse by Verse Bible Study
General Epistles: 1 Peter, 2 Peter, James

Pauline Epistles
Romans: The Just Shall Live by Faith
1 Corinthians: The Greatest of These is Love
2 Corinthians: My Grace is Sufficient for You
1 Thessalonians, 2 Thessalonians, Philemon
Pastoral Epistles: 1 Timothy, 2 Timothy, Titus
Galatians: Justified by Faith in Jesus Christ

Prison Epistles
The Prison Epistles
Philippians: Rejoice Always in the Lord
Colossians: He is the Image of the Invisible God
Ephesians: Every Spiritual Blessing in the Heavenly Places in Christ

Standalone
Apocalypse: Understanding the Book of Revelation
Expository Preaching
Memoirs of a Doctor
Moses: Let My People Go
The ABCS of Self-Publishing

Watch for more at https://www.drandrewcskoh.com.

About the Author

Dr. Andrew C S Koh published his first autobiography in 2020. Since then, he has published 40 Christian non-fiction novels, Bible Study guides, and devotionals on all books in the New Testament and 5 in the Old Testament. He is a cardiologist, author, publisher, blogger, podcaster, and bible teacher, He studied theology at Laidlaw College, Auckland, New Zealand.

Andrew makes his home in Malaysia with his family and enjoys coffee, traveling, and photography.

Find out more about Andrew on:

https://linktr.ee/andrewcskoh

Search Andrew's books on:

https://books2read.com/ap/xX066D/Dr-Andrew-C-S-Koh

get your free books here:

https://storyoriginapp.com/giveaways/b295be58-7736-11ec-ac4b-e34d930c508e

https://books2read.com/u/3kYJlN

Read more at https://www.drandrewcskoh.com.

About the Publisher

for more information on the publisher, check out;
https://www.drandrewcskoh.com